M O Z A R T

FOR ETIENNE, RITA, ADRIEN DELESSERT

Copyright © 1988 Editions La Joie de Lire, Geneva
Copyright © 1990 Creative Education Inc.
123 South Broad Street, Mankato, MN 56001, USA
For the American Edition.

International Copyrights reserved in all countries
Printed in Italy.

Library of Congress Cataloging-in-Publication Data

Mitchell, Barbara, 1941–
    Mozart / by Christopher Gallaz: adapted for the American reader
by Barbara Mitchell.
        p. cm.
    Summary: Imaginary letters from Mozart to the reader present
highlights of his life.
        ISBN 0-88682-322-6
        1. Mozart, Wolfgang Amadeus, 1756–1791—Juvenile literature.
    2. Composers—Austria—Biography—Juvenile literature.
    3. Imaginary letters—Juvenile literature.   [1. Mozart,
Wolfgang Amadeus, 1756–1791—Juvenile literature.
    2. Composers.]   I. Gallaz, Christophe, 1948–.   II. Title.
ML3930.M9M59   1990
780′.92—dc20   90-1326
[B]   CIP
[92]   AC MN

$\mathcal{M}$ O Z A R T

ILLUSTRATIONS BY
GEORGES LEMOINE
STORY BY
CHRISTOPHE GALLAZ

ADAPTED BY BARBARA MITCHELL
TRANSLATED BY PATRICIA HAUDUROY

CREATIVE EDUCATION INC.

My name is Wolfgang Amadeus Mozart. I write to you from Vienna, music capitol of the world. It is the month of September, 1791, and I am thinking about my life. I have traveled through all of Europe. I have performed for the empress, for the pope, for princes and princesses, for the king. I have won medals and honors. I have been kicked out of court. Audiences have adored me . . . and ignored me. I am asking. What is the meaning of it all? What is the sense of our successes and our failures? Of our loves? Will death erase them every one?

I am not a philosopher. I write quite ordinary letters to my family. It is in letter writing that I can be the joker. I like to make light of life. I sometimes sign my name in funny ways. Mozart hides his true feelings in his jokes, it has been said. Perhaps that is so. Only in my music can I express what moves me deeply.

In the golden light of summer's end, here in the wooden cabin by the theatre directed by my friend Emmanuel Schikaneder, I am preparing for the opening of my opera *The Magic Flute*. I tell of the fight between good and evil through two young people, Tamino and Pamina. The Queen of the Night will use them to destroy Sarastro, the spirit of wisdom. Look. I shall show you the scenery, the characters and the symbols of the opera.

"If we make a fiasco, I cannot help it," I said to Schikaneder when he presented me with the libretto. I had never written a "magic" opera before. The exotic story and eastern setting were strange to me. And yet, I felt at home. The opera is full of Masonic symbolism.

I think of my years as a Freemason. The Masons are a society dedicated to brotherhood and charity. Our history is a long one. Its roots go back to ancient Egypt, where "initiated ones" sought to make the world a more just place. In the 13th century, European masons—those workers in stone whose cathedrals touch the sky—took up the brotherhood. The movement grew. Masonry is international now.

Beneath *The Magic Flute*'s seemingly innocent fairy tale lie dangerous thoughts. I have written for Sarastro a grand aria. He sings of brotherhood. Today, at the end of the 18th century, brotherhood and equality are revolutionary ideas. "Liberty, Fraternity, Equality!" the French Revolutionists cry. Eloquent speech flows, and so does blood. It is in such a world that I compose my music. I feel within myself, in the mirror of my art, the hope for a world where love will triumph.

Glory to you, the initiated ones. You have vanquished the night.
Our gratitude to you, Isis, our gratitude to you, Osiris!
The forces of good have triumphed and
crowned beauty and wisdom for eternity.
THE MAGIC FLUTE

Operas, arias for theatre and concert, solos, duos, trios, quartets, quintets. Church sonatas, cantatas, oratorios, masses, Marches, dances, serenades, divertimentos, concertos, symphonies! I have composed more than six-hundred pieces for the complete range of the human voice and all the instruments of my time. Do my audiences hear them with their hearts as well as with their ears?

How well I remember the Duke de Chabot and his Duchess. The Duchess had behaved very haughtily, keeping me sitting in her cold drawing room. When at last I was asked to play, she chattered unceasingly with her guests. The Duke sat himself down beside me and listened attentively, and I forgot the cold and my headache and played as I play when I am in the mood. The Duke was one who understood.

I shall be understood and scorned. I shall be admired and detested. How, then shall I be remembered a hundred years from now? The futile composer of light melodies? How fifty years from that: the towering genius of harmony? None of this is important. Things fall into place gradually. I dare not bury this talent for composition which a kind God gave me in such measure. My life's pulse is music!

—*Wolfgang Amadeo*

September has turned to October. I have been to Prague for a festival performance of my opera *Don Giovanni*. These past two nights I have conducted the opening performances of *The Magic Flute*. Sadly, I must give up the baton. I am so tired. My headaches grow worse. I know. My traveling and performing days are done.

I see myself as a child: little Mozart with his tiny powdered wig and tiny violin. Childhood for my sister Nannerl and me was one long concert tour. We Mozarts traveled Europe like a family of acrobats. I was only six when we left Salzburg. Vienna, Manheim, Frankfurt, Brussels, Paris, London. The Hague, Amsterdam, Lyon, Geneva, Rome. So many concerts at capitols and courts! By the time I was fifteen, I had traveled 2500 miles and composed twenty symphonies, two operas, five masses, and many pieces for Nannerl and me on clavichord and violin.

Papa felt it his duty to exhibit his miracle child. And, he sensed my passion for music. His life's ambition was to secure for me a position as Konzertmeister. Serving as concertmaster for a nobleman was the way to success, he believed. Papa. He possesses me yet. As musicians we had great respect for one another. In personality, we were miles apart.

At sixteen I was named Konzertmeister to Count Girolamo Colloredo, Prince Archbishop of Salzburg. Colloredo expected me to turn out music on command, much as his cook turned out three meals a day. He commissioned only church music. I wanted to experiment with other musical forms. I traveled more and more frequently. The Archbishop was not pleased.

I was at court in Vienna, at the very center of musical life, in the spring of 1781 when Colloredo ordered me back to Salzburg. I would *not* bow and scrape to nobility, I declared. Papa and I had a furious argument. When I attempted to resign, Colloredo refused to see me. At last his chamberlain accepted my written resignation. With a boot in the pants, he propelled me out the door. I was free!

None but the whims of fate could control me now. I stayed in Vienna, composing my concertos for piano and orchestra. Beauty flowed from my pen. "Popularity is short-lived in Vienna," the old chamberlain had warned. Thoughts of poverty and wounded pride did not alarm me. I had overcome them in Paris, had I not?

Ah Paris, brilliant and cruel capitol, so often present in my memories. For my second visit there, I left Salzburg in September, 1777, alone with my mother. Much to our surprise, the welcome was lukewarm. No longer was I the child exhibited as a freakish prodigy in fashionable drawing rooms. I received only a few commissions for music. Often the payment was no more than a golden trinket. So many gold watches did I receive, that I threatened to drape myself with them for performances. Even playing in private became difficult. The drafty apartment we rented from a German scrap-iron dealer was too small for a keyboard instrument.

Mama, whose spirit was always turned towards Salzburg, became ill, and after three weeks in bed, died on July 3rd. "Your little dog Bimperl waits at the door for you each day," Nannerl wrote. I left Paris at the end of September. I have never returned.

Always during my travels, I spent time discovering the music of others. As a small boy I sat with Johann Christian Bach at the organ in London. The son of the great Johann Sebastian placed me between his knees and we took turns playing. In Paris I was inspired by Johann Schobert. In Bologna, Father Martini. I composed symphonies in the style of Italian overtures. Ancient Italian and Austrian melodies contributed to my developing style. I have always found the popular folk melodies scorned by the academics intriguing.

What joy it was to bring home precious scores of J. S. Bach from the Prussian court! Bach (dead now thirty-two years) took me back to the past with his clear style and disciplined composition.

It is Haydn who pushes me forward to a future rich in flowing melodies. Dear "Papa Haydn," twenty-four years my senior. It is lonesome here with my musical soul mate off to London for a year. I console myself with work: the Clarinet Concerto in A, for my friend Anton Stadler.

—Amadé

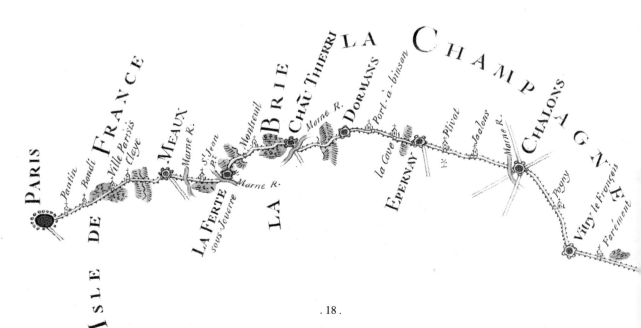

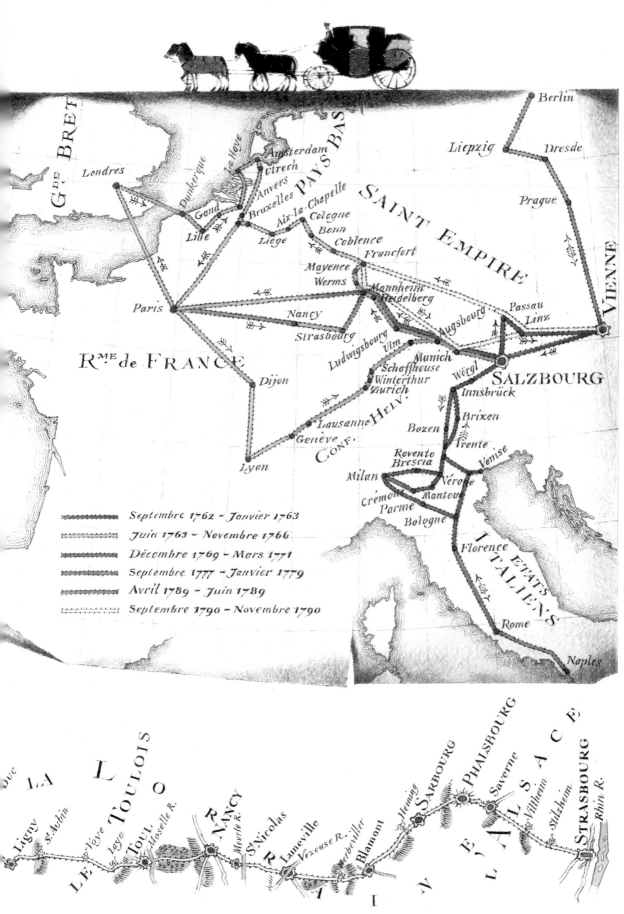

Gⁿᵉ BRET

Londres

Dunkerque
La Haye
Amsterdam
Utrech
Gand
Anvers
Bruxelles PAYS BAS
Lille
Aix-la-Chapelle
Liège
Cologne
Bonn
Coblence
Mayence
Francfort
Worms
Mannheim
Heidelberg
Nancy
Paris
Strasbourg
Ludwigsbourg
Ulm
Augsbourg
Passau
Linz
Munich
Wörgl
Schaffhouse
Winterthur
Zurich
Innsbrück
Dijon
Lausanne HELV.
Genève CONF.
Bozen
Brixen
Lyon
Trente
Rovento
Brescia
Venise
Milan
Vérone
Crémone
Mantoue
Parme
Bologne
Florence

SAINT EMPIRE

Berlin
Liepzig
Dresde
Prague
VIENNE

SALZBOURG

Rᵐᵉ de FRANCE

ÉTATS ITALIENS

Rome

Naples

	Septembre 1762 – Janvier 1763
	Juin 1763 – Novembre 1766
	Décembre 1769 – Mars 1771
	Septembre 1777 – Janvier 1779
	Avril 1789 – Juin 1789
	Septembre 1790 – Novembre 1790

Ligny
St Aubin
LA L O TOULOIS
DUC
LE Voye
Laye
TOUL
Mosella R.
NANCY
Meurte R.
S. Nicolas
Lunéville
Vezouse R.
Blamont
Henning
SARBOURG
PHALSBOURG
Saverne
Wilhem
ALSACE
Silzheim
STRASBOURG
Rhin R.

The scarlets and golds of autumn do little to lift my spirits. Tonight I sold my horse. I needed the handful of coins. I said "Good-bye"—then sent for black coffee and orchestrated the third movement of the clarinet concerto. Stadler owes me money. No matter. He is a faithful friend.

I dream of my early years in Vienna, happiest of my life. Oh, the parties, the musicales, the elegant clothes I so dearly love. It is as the chamberlain predicted. The fickle Viennese adored me and my music. Quite suddenly, their love turned cold. When my opera *The Abduction from the Seraglio* opened, the city was divided. Some applauded me. Others gathered around Antonio Salieri, the Italian musician who is Court Composer to Emperor Joseph. Salieri could have helped me. Instead, he plotted against me to strengthen his position at court. I am wounded, and at the same time, indifferent.

I shall have a game of billiards with that fellow who composed *The Magic Flute*. Then I shall write to my Constanze.

Here is Constanze, looking out the window of our apartment on the Schulerstrasse in Vienna. We were married on August 4, 1782. It was the first and only time I disobeyed my father. He found Constanze unworthy to be my wife. Am I some sort of God? I need to love, like anyone else. Constanze and I are like two happy children, Nannerl says.

In the beginning, we lived quite comfortably, inviting our many friends to play and eat and drink with us. Then on June 17, 1783, at six-thirty in the morning, Constanze gave birth to little Raimund-Leopold. It was the beginning of sorrows for us. Our precious son lived for just two months. Only two of our six children have survived: Karl-Thomas, seven years old now, and Franz-Xavior-Wolfgang, born this past July.

The years have gone by. Our luck has not improved. When I succeeded Christoph Willibald Gluck in 1781 as Royal and Imperial Court Musician, I received only half his revenue. We have had to move to a poorer neighborhood. We rarely entertain. Our silver has found its way to the pawn shop. Constanze is often exhausted and takes the baths at Baden.

—*Wolfgang et Amadeus Mozartus*

Gray November has been with us for three weeks now. *The Magic Flute* is a great success. I follow the performances moment by moment, playing out the themes on my pillow. I have taken to my bed. Fainting spells and nausea overwhelm me. My hands and feet are quite swollen. I have not been to the theatre since that night I played the glockenspiel part from the wings, deliberately coming in off beat. What fun!

Opera, the joy of my life! I like to be carried away by this unique marriage of language, music, and staging that creates a dramatic image of life. I really could weep whenever I hear an aria beautifully sung. Too often opera singers have only the opportunity to perform difficult feats rather than express heartfelt emotion. It is said that I have a gift for composing for the human voice. I only know that I seek a style without affectation: smooth melodies, fluidity of movement. Simplicity that expresses the passions of the human soul is my goal.

Mithridatis, Lucio Silla, Idomeneo, Abduction from the Seraglio, The Marriage of Figaro, Don Giovanni, Cosi fan Tutte, The Clemency of Titus, The Magic Flute. My operas, my life. Oh that I could go on composing opera forever. But I must concentrate on works that bring in money quickly. I am in the midst of a most mysterious assignment, a "Requiem" commissioned by an unknown person. A funeral mass. I am seized by such wretchedness that I sometimes fear it may be my own.

—*Gnagflow Trazom*

It is the fourth of December. I work almost desperately on the "Requiem." It tires me so that I feel my energy ebbing away onto the paper. And always there is the mysterious stranger reappearing at my door and asking, "Is it finished?"

Tonight we held an informal rehearsal session. Three friends joined in. I sang the alto. When we came to the *Lacrimosa,* I broke down and wept. The idea that this unfinished work is my own death music possesses me. Who is it that dares to haunt me in this way? Could it be a final plot of Salieri's? I feel so terribly ill that I wonder if I have been poisoned.

My emotions overtake me. I am distraught, hopelessly weak. Constanze helps me to my bed. She and her sister Sophie keep watch over me. The clock strikes twelve . . . A new day is dawning, and I am scarcely aware of it. I am weightless . . . fading, fading. They shall bury me in St. Mark's cemetary where the city shall ignore me . . .

—*Mozarty*

I am looking at you. Do you listen to my works at concerts, at the opera, on your records, your radio and your tapes? Through the centuries, many artists have hailed me as a very great genius. I do not know if they are right. I do not really care. I have put my whole being into my work, the joys and the sorrows. My music is both simple and complex, as are your days, as will be your life. It has the power to refresh you, strengthen you. My music listens to you. Do you listen to me?

—*Mozart*

Anna-Maria   Leopold   Wolfgang   Nannerl   Constanze

Wolfgang Amadeus Mozart was born on January 27, 1756 in Salzburg. His parents, Leopold and Anna-Maria, had seven children, but only Wolfgang and his older sister "Nannerl" survived. In 1782, in Vienna, Wolfgang married Constanze Weber. Only two of their six children survived, and they had no children themselves. Mozart was just 35 when he died on December fifth, 1791. The legend of the Salieri poisoning has been proven false. Medical scholars feel that his death was due to either rheumatic fever or kidney disease. He never knew that the "Requiem" had been commissioned through a middleman by a nobleman who wished to dedicate it to his wife and pass it off as his own.

S O M E   W O R K S

Five minuets for clavichord, K.1 to 5
Sonatas for clavichord with violin accompaniment, K.6 and 7
Twelve variations for piano in C maj. K.265;
"Ah, I Shall Tell You, Mama."
Twelve variations for piano in E flat maj. K.353;
"The Beautiful Frances."
Sonata for piano, No.11, in A maj. K.331
Sonatas for piano and violin K.55 to 59
Concerto for piano, No.20, in D minor, K.466
Concerto for piano, No.21, in C maj K.467
Concerto for bassoon and orchestra in E flat maj. K.191
Concerto for clarinet and orchestra in A. Maj. K.622
Serenade for 13 wind instruments, No.10, in B flat maj. K.361
Divertimento in D maj. K.251
Symphony N°33, in B flat maj. K.319
Symphony N°36, in C maj. K.425 "Linz"
High mass in C minor K.427
Masonic hymn in F maj. K.623a "Let's join our hands."
"Abduction from the Seraglio" K.384
"The Magic Flute" K.620

I would like to thank the friends who have helped me:
Annick Campin, Michèle and Jean Claverie, Basile Crichton
and les Editions Alphonse Leduc, Jean-Marie Curti, Florence Dollfus,
Maurice Garnier, Catherine Lootvoet, Annie and Joachim Nettelbeck,
Christine and Jean-Marie Perre, Françoise Robin, Eric Turmel.

G. L.